"We adore you,
O Christ,
and we bless you,
for by your holy cross
you have redeemed
the world."

*(Prayer from
the Stations of the Cross)*

*To my most
wonderful and beautiful father,
whom I miss
more than words
could ever express.*

—*R. S.*

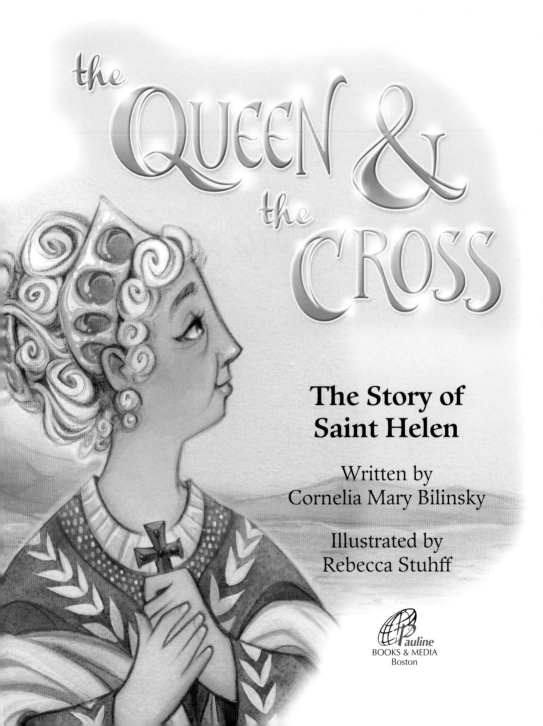

the QUEEN & the CROSS

The Story of Saint Helen

Written by
Cornelia Mary Bilinsky

Illustrated by
Rebecca Stuhff

Pauline
BOOKS & MEDIA
Boston

Library of Congress Cataloging-in-Publication Data

Bilinsky, Cornelia Mary.
The Queen and the Cross : The Story of Saint Helen / Written by Cornelia Mary Bilinsky.
pages cm -- (Tales and Legends)
ISBN-13: 978-0-8198-7461-0
ISBN-10: 0-8198-7461-2
1. Helena, Saint, ca. 255-ca. 330. 2. Holy Cross--Legends. I. Title.
BR1720.H4B55 2012
270.1092--dc23
[B]

    2012000666

ISBN: 08198-7461-2

Design by Mary Joseph Peterson, FSP

Published by Pauline Books & Media, 50 Saint Pauls Avenue, Boston, MA 02130-3491

Printed in Korea

QAC SIPSKOGUNKYO4-10024 7461-2

www.pauline.org

Pauline Books & Media is the publishing house of the Daughters of St. Paul, an international congregation of women religious serving the Church with the communications media.

1 2 3 4 5 6 7 8 9   16 15 14 13

Dear Lord

Jesus Christ,
as we look upon
your holy cross,
grant us the grace
to see clearly what Saint Helen saw when at last
she found the precious wood on which you so
willingly gave your life: the great love in your
outstretched arms,
the deep sorrow
in your sacred heart
because of our sins,
forgiveness whispered
through dying lips,
and the promise that
this was not the end
but the beginning,
the dawn of your
holy resurrection
and new life for all
of us. Help us to treasure
your cross above all things,
and honor it in all the small
crosses you ask us to carry as we follow you.

Amen.

All Christians know that Jesus died on the cross a long, long time ago. And all Christians know that Jesus was taken down from the cross, buried in a tomb, and on the third day rose again to new life. But does anyone know what happened to the cross on which Jesus died?

Queen Helen finished her evening prayers but remained standing with her hands clasped. Her eyes were fixed on the wooden cross hanging beside her bed. It had been given to her by the priest who had baptized her fifteen years before. Since that day, Queen Helen had faithfully offered her daily prayers before the cross. It gave her great comfort to see it, to touch it, and to kiss it.

Tonight, however, the elderly queen felt very restless. Something was on her mind and would not go away.

This cross is very precious to me, she thought, *but the* true *cross on which Jesus died is even more precious! How I would love to kiss the wood on which my Savior gave his life!*

When she finally went to bed, Queen Helen had made up her mind. *I will go to the Holy Land and search for the holy cross!*

With the blessing of her son, the Emperor Constantine, Queen Helen made her preparations. She gathered a company of good friends and workers. Together they set sail on a journey from Rome to Palestine. After many days, they arrived in Jerusalem.

Immediately Queen Helen went to visit Bishop Macarius, the leader of the Christian church in Jerusalem.

"I have come to find the cross on which Jesus died" she announced.

"It's been three hundred years since Jesus was crucified!" Macarius said. "His cross was lost long ago. . . ."

"Then we must start looking for it!" the queen insisted.

The bishop smiled. "Perhaps you should begin your search on Mount Calvary. That is where Jesus died."

Just outside the city walls, Queen Helen and her company began to climb up Mount Calvary. It was a very tiring climb, and Queen Helen kept thinking all the while how difficult it must have been for Jesus to carry his cross up this same steep hill.

When they reached the top, Queen Helen looked around in dismay. Everywhere there were huge piles of rubble, broken bricks, stones, sand, and dirt.

"With all this rubbish, how do you expect us to find a cross that was lost three hundred years ago?" the workers complained.

"We'll have to dig until we find it," Queen Helen answered.

"But where should we begin?" they asked. "Every-thing is in ruins!"

Queen Helen walked around the site.

"Dear God," she prayed, "help me find the precious cross, the true cross of Jesus."

Just then she noticed something. A small green plant was growing bravely at the base of one of the piles of rubbish. Queen Helen pinched off a leaf and examined it closely. It gave off a sweet spicy smell.

"I know what this is!" she said. "This is sweet basil, the herb of kings."

Remembering that Jesus is the King of Life, Queen Helen suddenly felt quite certain that the cross of Jesus was somewhere beneath that pile of rubble.

"Dig here," she said to the men.

The labor was long and hard. After many days of digging, the workers found something. They ran into the city to tell Queen Helen their news.

"Have you found the cross?" the queen asked eagerly.

"No, we found *three* crosses!" said the men.

"Of course!" cried Queen Helen, with excitement. "When Jesus was crucified, there were two thieves crucified with him, one on his left and the other on his right. I believe we have found our lost treasure!"

Queen Helen rushed to tell Bishop Macarius what had been discovered. Together they hurried back up to Mount Calvary.

There were indeed three crosses. The workers had brushed off the sand and dirt and laid them side by side on a mound.

"They all look the same!" Queen Helen exclaimed in distress. "How can we know which one is the cross of Jesus? There is supposed to be a marker that reads 'Jesus of Nazareth, King of the Jews.'"

"It is missing." said Macarius. "This is a mystery indeed! But I have an idea. There is a Christian family in Jerusalem whose youngest daughter has become gravely ill. The family is at her bedside at this moment, expecting that she will die soon. Let us take all three crosses to her. If one of them is truly the cross of Jesus, perhaps it will save her."

Queen Helen recalled how Jesus had healed the sick, the blind, and the crippled, and had brought the dead back to life. "Yes," she agreed, "let's go quickly."

The three crosses were
brought down into the city
of Jerusalem to the home of
the dying girl. The bishop spoke to the family
and explained his purpose. In a few moments
the girl was brought out on a stretcher and
laid down on the street. A crowd of onlookers
gathered around.

Everyone could see that the girl was near death. The bishop took one of the crosses and touched the sick girl with it. The crowd grew silent, waiting for something to happen. The girl lay in a coma, as before. Then the bishop did the same with the second cross. But the girl remained white and still, as if she were already dead.

"It's no use!" cried the mother. "She's dying! These old crosses will not help her! Leave us alone!"

"Wait! There is still hope!" Queen Helen called out. "There is one more cross!"

The bishop picked up the last cross and gently lowered it. As soon as the wood touched the sick girl, her body began to tremble. Suddenly, she opened her eyes, sat up, and looked around at all the people.

"What are you all doing here?" she asked in surprise.

The mother threw her arms around her daughter, kissing her over and over again. Everyone laughed and cried, amazed to see the dying girl restored to health.

Queen Helen sank to her knees. There were tears in her eyes. "I have found the treasure I have been looking for!" she cried joyfully. "I have found the true cross of Jesus!" Reverently she bowed down and kissed the foot of the cross.

Bishop Macarius raised the cross high into the air. "Good Christian people of Jerusalem," he declared. "This life-giving cross you see before you is the very same cross on which our Lord and Savior Jesus Christ suffered and died!"

All the people bowed down before the cross, praising and thanking God.

At that moment, Queen Helen knew what she would do. She would see to it that a beautiful church was built over the very spot on Mount Calvary where the cross had been found. Then pilgrims from all over the world could come to Jerusalem, as she had, and kneel before the cross to thank Jesus for his love.

Queen Helen returned home with a happy heart, taking with her only a small piece of the true cross. She cherished her new-found treasure for the rest of her days and gladly shared it with all who believed in the resurrection of Jesus Christ.

Today, wood from the holy cross is honored in Rome at the Basilica of the Holy Cross in Jerusalem, the monastery of Saint Toribio de Liébana in Spain, cathedrals and shrines throughout Europe, and at the Cathedral of the Holy Cross in Boston, U.S.A.

25

Saint Helen

*A*s a young girl, Saint Helen likely had no idea that she would one day be a queen, let alone a saint! Born around 250 in Bythnia (modern day Turkey), Helen was an innkeeper's daughter. At the age of twenty, while working as a stable maid, she met and married a Roman general, Constantius Chlorus. Together they had a son, Constantine. Constantine later became the Roman Emperor who ended the persecution of Christians and made faith in Christ legal.

Because of her humble beginnings, Helen was considered by the Romans to be an unsuitable wife for an important general. She and Constantius divorced. When her son, Constantine, was proclaimed Emperor (306), Helen moved to Rome, where she became a Christian (around 312). Constantine was very fond of his mother and honored her with the title of Augusta, which would be much the same as Queen. Helen was allowed to use the riches of the empire to help the poor and needy and to build churches.

Around 327, when she was almost eighty years old, Helen made a pilgrimage to the Holy Land to visit the places where Jesus had lived, suffered, and died. According to legend, it was during that pilgrimage that the three crosses were uncovered on Mount Calvary, and the true cross of Jesus was identified. On the site of the discovery, a magnificent church was built. The *Church of the Holy Sepulcher* or the *Church of the Resurrection,* as it is named by Eastern Christians, still stands there today.

It is believed that most of the true cross remained in Jerusalem and a portion was sent to Rome. Helen's palace in Rome was converted to the *Basilica of the Holy Cross in Jerusalem*. Relics of the cross can still be seen there.

Helen died in the year 330. Her feast day is celebrated on August 18. The Feast of the Exaltation of the Holy Cross is celebrated on September 14. Bishop Macarius of Jerusalem is also a saint. He is remembered on March 10.

" . . . it is fitting that the most marvelous place in the world should be worthily decorated."

(Letter of the Emperor Constantine to Bishop Macarius of Jerusalem, about the church to be built on Mount Calvary)

Cornelia Mary Bilinsky was born and raised in Manitoba. She received her bachelor of arts degree in English and theology from St. Paul's College at the University of Manitoba. She taught English at the high school level as well as English as a second language at a community college. Cornelia's husband is a Ukrainian Catholic priest. They currently reside in Oshawa, Ontario, and have one daughter and one granddaughter. Since 1981, Cornelia has worked alongside her husband at Ukrainian Catholic parishes in Ontario. She most enjoys teaching children about the faith with stories, plays, and songs. Cornelia is the author of *Santa's Secret Story* and *The Saint Who Fought the Dragon* (Pauline Kids, 2011) and *The Queen and the Cross* (2013).

Rebecca Stuhff started drawing as soon as she was able to hold a pencil and hasn't stopped since. She earned a bachelor of fine arts in illustration from Utah Valley University. Rebecca enjoys traveling and has actually seen Saint Helen's sarcophagus on display in the Vatican Museum, as well as many mosaics and sculptures of Saint Helen and her son Constantine in Rome. You can see more of her artwork on the web by visiting RebeccaStuhff.com.

Tales and Legends from

Pauline kids

The 3 Trees
Adapted by Gabriel Ringlet
Illustrated by Daniella Oh

The Little Lost Lamb
Written and Illustrated by Geri Berger Haines

the QUEEN & the CROSS
The Story of Saint Helen
Written by Cornelia Mary Bilinsky
Illustrated by Rebecca Stuhff

SANTA'S Secret Story
Written by Cornelia Mary Bilinsky
Illustrated by Candace Camling

The Saint Who Fought the Dragon
The Story of Saint George
Written by Cornelia Mary Bilinsky
Illustrated by Theresa Brandon

Who are the Daughters of St. Paul?

We are Catholic sisters. Our mission is to be like Saint Paul and tell everyone about Jesus! There are so many ways for people to communicate with each other. We want to use all of them so everyone will know how much God loves us. We do this by printing books (you're holding one!), making radio shows, singing, helping people at our bookstores, using the internet, and in many other ways.

Visit our Web site at www.pauline.org

BOOKS & MEDIA

The Daughters of St. Paul operate book and media centers at the following addresses. Visit, call or write the one nearest you today, or find us at www.pauline.org

CALIFORNIA
3908 Sepulveda Blvd, Culver City, CA 90230	310-397-8676
935 Brewster Avenue, Redwood City, CA 94063	650-369-4230
5945 Balboa Avenue, San Diego, CA 92111	858-565-9181

FLORIDA
145 S.W. 107th Avenue, Miami, FL 33174	305-559-6715

HAWAII
1143 Bishop Street, Honolulu, HI 96813	808-521-2731
Neighbor Islands call:	866-521-2731

ILLINOIS
172 North Michigan Avenue, Chicago, IL 60601	312-346-4228

LOUISIANA
4403 Veterans Memorial Blvd, Metairie, LA 70006	504-887-7631

MASSACHUSETTS
885 Providence Hwy, Dedham, MA 02026	781-326-5385

MISSOURI
9804 Watson Road, St. Louis, MO 63126	314-965-3512

NEW YORK
64 West 38th Street, New York, NY 10018	212-754-1110

PENNSYLVANIA
Philadelphia—relocating	215-676-9494

SOUTH CAROLINA
243 King Street, Charleston, SC 29401	843-577-0175

VIRGINIA
1025 King Street, Alexandria, VA 22314	703-549-3806

CANADA
3022 Dufferin Street, Toronto, ON M6B 3T5	416-781-9131

**"To Your Cross,
O Master,
we bow in veneration,
and we glorify
Your Holy Resurrection!"**

*(Hymn of the Eastern Church
on the Feast of the Exaltation
of the Holy Cross)*